SAMSUNG GALAXY TAB A USERS GUIDE

The Beginner to Expert Guide with Tips
And Tricks to Master Your Galaxy Tab A
10.1" 10.5" & 8.0" Like A Pro

John White

Contents

Introduction

It has been over two years since Samsung last upgraded its 10-inch entry-level Galaxy Tab A tablet. An update was necessary, especially regarding software.

The Galaxy Tab A 10.1 2019 is an ideal slate for enjoying digital content with a large and luscious display as well as sufficient horsepower and battery life for enjoying movies and web browsing on the go.

The Samsung Galaxy Tab A 10.1 2019 runs Android 9.0 Pie out of the box. In fact, it is the first tablet to ship with this version of Android.

In the case of the Galaxy Tab A 10.1 (2019), the software highlight of the new OneUI for tablets is not the new interface, but a feature with which the tablet offers additional added value. It is called *Smart Things* and turns a pure multimedia tablet into a smart home control center.

This software can be used to control smart home products from a wide range of manufacturers via a single interface. This saves you the hassle of switching back and forth between the different manufacturers apps. According to Samsung, it already supports about 400 products worldwide and not only those from their own line, but also from third-party vendors such as Philips Hue, Netgear Arlo, Ring and many more.

Setting up your tablet

These are the steps you need to go through to get the Galaxy Tab set up. There are a lot of steps, but don't worry, we'll take you through everything you need to do.

1. When you first turn the tablet on, you'll need to choose a language. Press

Start if you want to use the default 'English (United Kingdom)' or tap it to choose a different one.

2. Tap your network name to connect to Wi-Fi.

3. Type in your wireless password and tap Connect.

4. When it connects, the network name will be in blue and it'll say 'Connected'. Tap Next.

5. Read through the 'End user license agreement', then choose whether you want to send Diagnostic data to Samsung by ticking or un-ticking the box.

6. You'll need to agree to the 'Terms and Conditions' by tapping AGREE.

7. If you already have a Google account, enter your email address to sign in, otherwise choose Or create a new account.

8. You'll need a Google account for downloading things like apps and games from the Play Store. Type in your password, and then tap Next.

9. Tap Accept to agree to Google's 'Terms of Service' and 'Privacy Policy'.

10.   You can add 'Payment info' if you want, this makes it easier to buy apps and games through the Play store. Lots of apps are free so it isn't essential that you do this. You can skip it by tapping Remind me later.

11.   Check that the time and date are correct, then tap Next.

12.   If you've used Android before, you can restore your data from an old backup. Just tap the one you want to restore, or to set it up as a new tablet, tap Next.

13.   Google uses some services that run in the background. You can read about them

here, and choose which ones you want to use by ticking or un-ticking the boxes, then press Next.

14.   A   Samsung   account   lets   you use some other Samsung services. You can just use your Google account to sign in, or Skip if you're not interested.

15.   If you choose to Skip the Samsung account, tap Skip again and you'll be taken to the Home screen.

Touch buttons

Under the main screen there's a button in the middle, and a touch button on either side of it. Here's what they're for and what they do.

'Home' (circle): pressing this gets you back to the Home screen from any screen or app.

'Back' (triangle): takes you back one screen.

'Menu' (square): shows apps you've used before.

Connecting to the Internet

Lots of the Galaxy Tab features need the internet to work properly and you'll also need the internet to use things like email and social media.

1. Swipe down from the top of the screen to see the 'notification panel'.

2. Press and hold the Wi-Fi icon to go to the settings.

3. Make sure it's turned on, then tap the network name you want to connect to.

4. Type in the wireless password and tap Connect. If you're not sure what the password is, it's usually printed on your router.

When it's done, you'll see 'Connected' under the network name.

Setting up your email accounts

Your Galaxy Tab can manage lots of email accounts, and you probably added a Gmail account when you went through the original Setup, but here's how to add more.

1. Open the Settings and go to Accounts > Add account.
2. Choose Email, then type in the email address, tap Next.
3. Enter your password, and tap Next.
4. Choose your 'Sync' options by ticking or un-ticking the boxes, and press Next to finish adding the account.

The account will set up automatically and you'll be taken back to the settings page, where you'll see it listed. If it doesn't work, you might need to add the settings manually.

Setting up a lock screen

Protecting your tablet with a lock screen is a good idea, because it stops other people from using it without your permission. Here's how to set one up.

1. Go to Settings > Lock screen and security and choose Screen lock type.
2. Choose the type of lock you want to use - we recommend using 'PIN' or 'Password' because they're the most secure.
3. Type in the PIN or Password you want to use, then tap Continue.
4. Type it in again to confirm it, then press OK.

That's your lock screen set up, and you'll be taken back to the Home screen.

Samsung account

Your Samsung account is an integrated account service that allows you to use a variety of Samsung services provided by mobile devices, TVs, and the Samsung website. Once your Samsung account has been registered, you can keep your data up to date and secure across your Samsung devices with Samsung Cloud, track and control your lost or stolen device.

To check the list of services that can be used with your Samsung account, visit account.samsung.com. For more information on Samsung accounts, launch the Settings app and tap Accounts and backup> Accounts>Samsung account > Help.

Registering your Samsung account

If you do not have a Samsung account, you should create one.

1. Launch the Settings app and tap Accounts and backup>Accounts>   Add   account>Samsung account. Alternatively, launch the Settings app and tap 👤

2. Tap Create account.

3. Follow the on-screen instructions to complete creating your account.

Registering an existing Samsung account

If you already have a Samsung account, register it to the device.

1. Launch the Settings app and tap Accounts and backup>Accounts> Add account>Samsung account.

2. Enter your Samsung account ID and password and tap Sign in.

If you forget your account information, tap Find ID or Reset password. You can find your account information when you enter the required information.

3. Read and agree to the terms and conditions and tap Next to finish registering your Samsung account. If a pop-up window about using biometric data appears, tap Register.

You can verify your Samsung account password via your biometric data, such as fingerprints.

Removing your Samsung account

When you remove your registered Samsung account from the device, your data, such as contacts or events, will also be removed.

1. Launch the Settings app and tap Accounts and backup> Accounts.

2. Tap Samsung account>Remove account.

3. Tap Remove, enter your Samsung account password, and then tap OK

Transferring data from your previous device (Smart Switch)

Connect with your previous device via Smart Switch to transfer data. Launch the **Settings** app and tap **Accounts and backup** → **Smart Switch**.

- This feature may not be supported on some devices or computers.

- Limitations apply. Visit www.samsung.com/smartswitch for details. Samsung takes copyright seriously. Only transfer content that you own or have the right to transfer.

Transferring data wirelessly via Wi-Fi Direct

Transfer data from your previous device to your device wirelessly via Wi-Fi Direct.

- On the previous device, launch Smart Switch. If you do not have the app, download it from **Galaxy Store** or **Play Store**.

- On your device, launch the **Settings** app and tap **Accounts and backup** → **Smart Switch**.

- Place the devices near each other.

- On the previous device, tap **Send data** → **Wireless**.

- On the previous device, select an item to transfer and tap **Send**.

- On your device, tap **Receive**.

- Follow the on-screen instructions to transfer data from your previous device.

Transferring data using external storage

Transfer data using external storage, such as a microSD card.

- Transfer data from your previous device to external storage.
- Insert or connect the external storage device to your device.
- On your device, launch the **Settings** app and tap **Accounts and backup** → **Smart Switch**→ **Restore**.
- Follow the on-screen instructions to transfer data from external storage.

Transferring backup data from a computer

Transfer data between your device and a computer. You must download the Smart Switch computer version app from

www.samsung.com/smartswitch.   Back   up data
from your previous device to a computer and
import the data to your device.

- On the computer, visit
  www.samsung.com/smartswitch to
  download Smart Switch.
- On the computer, launch Smart Switch.

If your previous device is not a Samsung device,
back up data to a computer using a program
provided by the device's manufacturer. Then,
skip to the fifth step.

- Connect your   previous   device   to   the
  computer using the device's USB cable.
- On   the computer, follow   the   on-screen
  instructions to back up data from   the
  device. Then, disconnect your previous
  device from the computer.
- Connect your device to the computer using
  the USB cable.

- On the computer, follow the on-screen instructions to transfer data to your device.

Viewing imported data

You can view the imported data on the same app from your previous device.

If your new device does not have the same apps to view or play the imported data, the data will be saved to a similar app.

Indicator icons

Indicator icons appear on the status bar at the top of the screen. The icons listed in the table below are most common.

Icon	Meaning
⃠	No signal
ᵢᵢₗ	Signal strength
	Roaming (outside of normal service area)

R	
G ↓↑	GPRS network connected
E ↓↑	EDGE network connected
3G ↓↑	UMTS network connected
H ↓↑	HSDPA network connected
H+ ↓↑	HSPA+ network connected
4G ↓↑ / **LTE** ↓↑	LTE network connected
📶	Wi-Fi connected
✳	Bluetooth feature activated
📍	Location services being used
📞	Call in progress
☎	Missed call
💬	New text or multimedia message
⏰	Alarm activated
🔇	Mute mode activated

- The status bar may not appear at the top of the screen in some apps. To display the

17

status bar, drag down from the top of the screen.

- Some indicator icons appear only when you open the notification panel. Call-related features are not supported on some models.

Icon	Meaning
📳	Vibration mode activated
✈	Flight mode activated
⚠	Error occurred or caution required
🔋	Battery charging
🔋	Battery power level

Lock screen

Pressing the Power key turns off the screen and locks it. Also, the screen turns off and automatically locks if the device is not used for a specified period.To unlock the screen, swipe in any direction when the screen turns on.

If the screen is off, press the Power key or double-tap anywhere on the screen to turn on the screen.

Changing the screen lock method

To change the screen lock method, launch the **Settings** app, tap **Lock screen** → **Screen lock type**, and then select a method. When you set a pattern, PIN, password, or your biometric data for the screen lock method, you can protect your personal information by preventing others from accessing your device. After setting the screen lock method, the device will require an unlock code whenever unlocking it.

- **Swipe**: Swipe in any direction on the screen to unlock it.

- **Pattern**: Draw a pattern with four or more dots to unlock the screen.

- **PIN**: Enter a PIN with at least four

numbers to unlock the screen.

- **Password**: Enter a password with at least four characters, numbers, or symbols to unlock the screen.

- **None**: Do not set a screen lock method.

- **Face**: Register your face to unlock the screen.

- **Fingerprints**: Register your fingerprints to unlock the screen.

You can set your device to perform a factory data reset if you enter the unlock code incorrectly several times in a row and reach the attempt limit. Launch the **Settings** app, tap **Lock screen** → **Secure lock settings**, unlock the screen using the preset screen lock method, and then tap the **Auto factory reset** switch to activate it.

Remove Google Search bar

If you want to remove the Google Search bar, simply tap and hold the bar and a remove button will appear at top of the screen, drag the bar to that remove button, and the bar will disappear.

If this is not working, go to Settings – Applications – Application manager. Then swipe from right to left so you are on the All screen. Scroll to Google search and press Disable.

Use built in Torch / Flashlight

The most recent version of Android now comes with a built in Flashlight / Torch App.

To find this, simply pull down to see your notifications. Then on the top bar (where you see your settings for WiFi, Bluetooth etc.), scroll across until you see Torch.

How to setup a new email account

If you want to setup new email accounts, like Yahoo or Hotmail, go to your list of Apps. Find the Email icon and press on it. A setup wizard will then be launched.

Enter you email address and password into the fields. You can also change the settings after this step.

Once you're happy with the settings, give your account a Name and you're done.

How to Enable Developer Mode

If you want to access certain features of your device that are only available to developers, then you want the Developer options setting.

On most devices, this feature is hidden so you will need to pull down your notifications screen go into Settings. Then scroll down to About device.

Then you should see Build Number. This needs to be pressed a total of seven times. You should get a message at the fourth press. On the seventh, you'll get another message saying that Developer Options are unlocked.

Speed up your browser

You can speed up the page load speed on your browser by disabling JavaScript.

To do this, open your Browser, then press the Menu or More button and then Settings. Then select Advanced and change the Enable JavaScript option.

Please note that this may affect the functionality of some sites.

How to restrict Apps in the Play store

The Play store contains thousands of great Apps, but there are times that you want to restrict access to these Apps for whatever reasons. This can easily be done.

First, open the Play Store App and swipe from left to right to see the settings. Then press Settings and Content Filtering.

From here you can chose settings for Low/Medium/High maturity levels. Great for preventing access for young people.

Enable Power Saving mode

If you tend to run out of battery power quickly, then you can turn on Power saving mode.

Pull down the notification screen by swiping your finger from the top of the phone. Then select Power Saving. You may need to scroll along the available icons.

You can also select to turn on Battery saver automatically, once battery reaches at certain level. To enable this, go to Settings – Battery –

Battery saver, and then turn Automatic Battery Saver on.

View HTML source code of web pages

If you are browsing a website and want to see the HTML source code behind the page, then Android doesn't offer you the ability to do this by default.

There is however a handy App called View Web Source which can be installed. Whenever you want to view the HTML of a web page, you just press the Menu – Share – View Web Source.

You can then browse the code or copy the content into the clipboard.

Quickly block common notifications

If you find that a particular App is sending you too many notifications, there is a quick way to disable these.

When you receive the notification, pull down the notification screen. Then long press on the notification, then Go to Settings/More Settings, from here you can turn notifications ON or OFF for that particular App.

Quickly switch between Home/App screens

This tip is relatively obvious, but some users overlook it. Once you go into your Home/Apps screen you should see a row of dots. This indicates which of the 5 Home/App screens you are on. Rather than flick between each screen, you can simply press one of the dots and you will jump to that homescreen.

Or alternatively, slide your finger across the dots to move between screens.

Check phone status, battery usage, signal strength

To find out information about Signal Strength, Network Information, Remaining Battery Time and Battery Usage (by Application), drag down your notifications screen and select Settings. Then under System, select About device and choose Status.?

Use phone as a WiFi hotspot / USB / Bluetooth tethering

To use your phone as a WiFi hotspot, tether it via USB or via Bluetooth, then go to Settings – Wireless and Network – Mobile hotspot and tethering.

You can then choose from three options:

1) USB – connect your phone via a USB cable. The phone should automatically configure the correct settings.

2) Mobile/WiFi Hotspot – To turn your phone into a WiFi hotspot, press Configure WiFi hotspot. You will then be asked to enter a Network SSID (this is your own name for the WiFi hotspot). Then choose Security and lastly, choose a password (this is password for your WiFi hotspot which you will enter on your computer).

3) Bluetooth – With this option, you will need to pair a Bluetooth device with your phone. On the other device, ensure you search for Bluetooth devices and your phone should show up.

How to show the Android Easter egg

There is a hidden Android Easter egg on the phone that Google has built into your device.

Go to Settings. Then scroll down to About device. Then tap on the Android version option 5 times.

Once you see something on the screen, you can then rub the screen with your finger to produce another surprise. If rubbing doesn't work then try tapping with your finger. A combination of the above should work.

By the way don't expect to see an actual Easter Egg. That is just the name given to things hidden inside software or operating systems.

Make volume / music louder

WARNING: Making your volume or music louder can damage your hearing.

Most phones have their volumes limited by local laws to protect your hearing. There is a way to boost your volume however.

Go to the Play Store and download an App called Volume Booster or Volume+ FREE or Ultimate Volume Booster

You may need to Root your phone for this App to work, but read the instructions in the App's description.

How to fix homescreen lag / slowness

Depending on how your phone is set up, sometimes you will see lag when swiping between homescreens. There are a number of things you can try to fix this, as follows:

First, try restarting your phone. This will fix many problems.

If that doesn't work, then remove any Widgets that pull data to the phone, such as Twitter, Weather widgets etc.

If you have Live wallpapers turned on, then try turning them off by going to Settings – Wallpaper, then changing to a different Wallpaper.

Go to Settings – System – Developer options – Window Animation Scale and Transition Animation Scale. Try changing these to 0.5x (or even 0).

(you will need to unlock Developer options if you can't find this. Use the search form on this site).

Sometimes the problem can be with the phone or operators skin or launcher, so try going to the Play Store and downloading a third party launcher such as Nova launcher or Go LauncherEx. Note: you will need to re-create your homescreen shortcuts, but they are both great launchers.

Another tip is to always press the Back key instead of the Home key when leaving Apps. The Back key will often close the App properly, while the Home key can leave it running in the background.

Stop Photos or Music files being indexed

To stop the Photo App or the Music player from indexing your files, place a blank text file called .nomedia in the folder containing your photos or music.

The best way to do this is to connect your device to a PC and then navigate to the relevant folder via your PC.

Save a word to the dictionary

Type a word that is not in the dictionary. The word will show up in the suggestion box to the left. Long press on the word and it will save to the dictionary.

Change the backlight screen timeout

To change the backlight screen timeout, drag down your notifications screen and press Settings. Then under System select Display. Then under Screen timeout you can set the screen time out duration.

You can also tell the phone screen to always stay lit when it is plugged in via USB. Go to Settings – System – Developer Options. Then check Stay Awake.

Note: Developer Options is not always enabled by default. To enable, go to Settings – System – About Device. Then tap on Build number 7 times to enable this secret option.

Pair with Bluetooth speakers or headset

Here's how to pair your device with another Bluetooth device.

First you will need to turn Bluetooth on. To do this, drag your finger from the top of the screen down, to show your notifications menu. Then press Bluetooth so the icon is green.

Then press the Scan button and your device will start to scan for pairable devices.

Choose the desired device and press Accept. You may be asked to enter a PIN or Password.

Double tap to highlight a word

When entering text into Apps such as your Messaging App, Facebook App and so on, you can tap on the words to start selecting text. Normally, you would then drag the left and right sliders to select the word, or words you want to highlight.

If you double tap on a word however, it will quickly select that word. Very handy for quickly copying and one word, name or place.

Check the firmware version

To see which firmware version of Android you are using, use the pull-down menu by dragging your finger from the top of the phone. Select Settings and under System, choose About Device.? This should list your Android version, Build number and Model Number.

Auto focus the camera

When taking photos or videos, tap the screen where you want to focus on. The phone will automatically adjust the settings to improve the image or video

How to turn off predictive text

If you would prefer to correct your own mistakes, then go to Settings – System – Language and input. Then select the keyboard you are using and press the Settings icon again. You should be able to find a predictive text option on this screen.

How to change the screen brightness

To adjust your screen brightness, there are two options:

1) Simply drag your finger from the top of the phone down to pull down your quick settings screen. Then at the top there will be a brightness bar. Drag this left or right or press Auto.

2) Drag your notifications screen down and select Settings. Then under Device, select

Display – Brightness. Then choose the desired brightness setting.

You can also select Automatic brightness to let the phone decide for you.

How to find your IMEI address / number

There are a number of ways to get your IMEI number. First, you can go to Settings – System – About device – Status. Scroll down and you should see IMEI listed on the screen.

Secondly, often the box that your device came in will have the IMEI printed on the label of the box or on the invoice.

Thirdly, if your device has a removable battery then open the cover and remove the battery. Your IMEI should be on a serial number plate and your IMEI number should be shown there.

Lastly, from the Dialler, enter *#06# and it should be displayed on the screen. This won't work on all phones and all networks however.

Enable sideload of Apps

If you want to install Apps outside of the Play Store (called sideloading), then go to Settings – Personal – Lock screen and security and select Unknown sources.

This setting will allow you to download Apps onto your device that would normally be blocked in the Play store.

Note: use at your own risk.

Swipe left to text contact

While viewing your list of Contacts you can swipe from Right to Left to send a text message to the selected contact.

This might not work on all models.

Show content in immersive mode

Recent Android versions use a special mode that hides all Android related visuals. The mode is called immersive mode and it essentially means certain Apps have the whole screen available.

Sometimes this can be annoying however and you want to see the time, signal strength or battery indicator.

To temporarily leave immersive mode, simply drag down your notifications screen and the phone will exit immersive mode so you can see other features.

Reject certain calls

If you find yourself being stalked or receiving unwanted calls nuisance calls from people or companies then you should use the Call rejection mode.

Open your Dialler App and press More. Then Settings and More settings. Then find Call rejection. From here you can manage your rejection list of numbers.

Help, I have forgotten my unlock pattern

If you have forgotten your custom unlock pattern, then don't panic. After 5 unsuccessful tries a button should appear saying 'Forgot pattern'. Press this and you will be asked to enter your Gmail username/password.

The phone will then ask for a new unlock pattern. If you don't have a Gmail account, then you might have to either call your carrier or factory reset your phone.

Create folders in your Quick Launch bar

If you have used up all of your Quick Launch spaces, then there is a trick. Once it is full, press and drag an App from the homescreen and move it over the top of an App in the Quick Launch area. Then release your finger. This will create a folder containing the original App plus the new one. This is a great way to have access to regularly used Apps.

Once you have done this grouping, you can give specific name to that folder. For that just open the folder (containing different apps), and tap on Tools tab, and add your desired name.

Remove large applications

If you are running low on phone memory, you can look for your largest applications to uninstall.

Go to Settings – Applications – Application manager. Then swipe from right to left and select Running.

From here you can see which applications are taking up the most memory and close them.

Bookmark a web page on your homescreen

If you regularly visit a website you can add a shortcut to your homescreen which can be quite useful, rather than entering the web address each time you want to visit the site.

You can either do this to an existing Bookmark, or simply a page you're visiting:

1) Open your Browser App. Enter the website you want to bookmark. You may need to wait for the whole page to load first. Then press the phone's Menu button or More at the top and select Add shortcut to home screen.

2) Open your Browser App. Find an existing Bookmark by pressing the Bookmarks icon at the bottom of the App. Select the Bookmark and repeat the above steps.

Change quick response texts

The phone has the ability to send quick response text messages if your phone is ringing but you can't answer it.

To change these, go to your Dialler App and press the Menu or More button. Then select Settings – Call rejection.

From here you can add or edit your reject messages.

Double tap for a full stop (period)

While typing emails or notes, you can simply tap the space key twice and the phone will insert a full stop / period.

This option may need to be turned on in the keyboard settings. This can be found in Settings – System – Language and input

Have more control over your notification light

If you are not happy with your notification light, then you can change and tweak it. Go to the Play Store and download an App called Light Flow.

You might need to enable the notification light before the App works. Go to Settings – Device – Sounds and notifications – LED Indicator.

Alternatively, for some devices, you can turn? Your Notification Light 'ON or OFF' and you can also change the color of Notification Light. For that go to Settings – Display and then toggle pulse notification icon. You can change the color of LED light from same menu.

Quickly open settings

If you want to go to settings, then you can go to your list of Apps and open the Settings App.

There is however a quicker way. Simply position your finger right at the top of the screen and drag it down. You may need to do this twice on some phones.

Your notification bar will appear and you can then press the small Gear icon at the top of the screen to go to the Settings.

Swipe to clear individual notifications

A handy feature of Android is to quickly clear your notifications.

Simply pull down your notifications bar by swiping your finger from the top of your phone downwards.

Then when you see each individual notification, swipe your finger left or right to clear each one. You can do this with your Apps too – press and hold the multitasking button. Then swipe left or right to close Apps.

Allow swear words in voice recognition

By default, your phone will recognise swear words, but insert x's instead of the word. To change this, go to Settings – System – Language and input – Virtual Keyboard- Google Voice Typing

Then you may need to select your voice input system. Then toggle the Block offensive words option.

Quickly close Apps

To quickly close Apps, press the Home key. This will display your currently running Apps. From here you can simply swipe the Apps off the screen by dragging your finger left or right. This is a very quick way to free up some memory.

How to set / change wallpaper

To change the homescreen or lock screen wallpaper, press on a blank part of the homescreen. Next, choose Wallpapers.

From here you can use any image in your Gallery as your Wallpaper.

Alternatively Open any image from Gallery, and tap on More Button, from here you can select any image as Home Screen Wallpaper or Lock Screen Wallpaper.

How to remove Picasa albums from phone Gallery

Android cleverly uses Picasa to sync photos between your account and your phone. Sometimes however, this means that you will get duplicates appearing in your Gallery when they're not actually on your phone.

To stop this from happening, and so you only see photos on the Phone or SD card, then follow these steps:

Drag down your notification menu from the top and click on the Gear icon to bring up your Settings. Then select Accounts and Google. Then select your Gmail account.

You should see a list of options that are ticked. Scroll down to the one that refers to Picasa and untick that.

Now that's done we want to remove the thumbnails from your Gallery, so we need to refresh the Gallery. To do that, swipe down and go to Settings again. Then select More – Application Manager. Swipe across to show ALL Apps. Then find the Gallery App and press Clear Data.

This will erase the thumbnails in your Gallery, so don't panic that your photos have disappeared. Just wait for the Gallery to re-build its index which could take awhile.

But the good news is that your Picasa Albums shouldn't be there anymore.

Change your Contact list order / sort by Last Name

If you don't like the default A-Z way of viewing your contacts you can change this.

First, go to your Contacts App and press the Menu key or More at the top of the screen. Then select Settings. Then choose Sort by.

Silence the tab when ringing

To silence the tab when ringing there are two methods:

Either press the Volume Down (or Up) button or if the phone is on a surface facing up, simply flip it over so it is facing down.

How to disable the screen lock

If you don't want to have to unlock your screen every time you take your device out of standby then go to Settings – Personal – Lock screen and security. Then select Screen lock type and select None.

How to hard reset / factory reset

Warning: This will remove ALL data on the tab (but not the MicroSD card). To perform a hard reset, or factory reset, then there are a number of methods to try:

1. Go to Settings – Personal – Backup and reset – Factory data reset – Reset device. It may ask for a password. Then select Erase everything.

If the phone is totally unresponsive, even after a reboot, then try the following methods.

2. While the tab is turned off, press and hold the Volume Up and Volume Down buttons together. Then, while holding these, press and release the Power button (keep holding the volume buttons). The tab should turn on and a menu will appear. Press the Volume down button to navigate to the Recovery option. Press the Volume Up to select (if that doesn't work, use the Power button to select). A yellow triangle and an Android logo will appear. Press the Volume Down and Volume Up button together and a recovery menu should appear. Use the Volume buttons to move to the Wipe data/Factory reset option and then press Power to select. Again, use the Volume Down key to choose Yes and press the Power button again to select.

3. While the tab is turned off, press and hold the Volume Down button. Then, while holding, press

and release the Power button. A menu should appear. Use the Volume down key to go to Clear Storage. Use the Power button to select the option. Then when asked to confirm, press Volume Up for Yes.

4. While the tab is off, press and hold down Volume Up + Home + Power buttons at the same time. Then release the buttons when you see the Logo. Use the Volume Down button to go down and the Home or Power key to select. Choose the Wipe data/Factory reset option. Then Select Yes to delete all user data. Then choose to reboot the phone.

5. A final method is to enter the code into your phone's dialler: *2767*3855# This method will not give you an option to reverse the process, so be careful! This method will only work if you can boot into your phone.

Enable / disable notification light

To enable / disable your notification light, go to Settings – Device – Sounds and notifications – LED indicator. From here you can choose various options.

This may not be available on all models. An alternative however is to download NoLED from the Play Store, which has many options for incoming notifications.

Move widgets between homescreens

If you want to move a widget from one homescreen to another, simply press and hold on the widget. Then drag it to the edge of the screen. The next homescreen will appear. Then, just drag the item to where you would like.

Use Swipe for quick text entry

Most Android devices come with an alternative way of entering text called Swype. Many prefer this method and believe it is quicker.

When any text entry box appears, press and hold the box. Then select Input method: SWYPE. Once enabled, you simply drag your finger around the keyboard moving over the letters in the correct order to spell a word.

Swipe right to dial contact

From the Contact list or the Messaging list, swipe from Left to Right to call a Contact. This might not work on all models.

Keep screen on when USB plugged in

Sometimes you may need your screen to stay on when plugged in via USB.

To do this, Drag down your notifications screen and press Settings. Then under System, select Developer Options. Then check Stay Awake.

If you can't see Developer options then you need to enable this. Go to Settings – System – About device and press on Build number 7 times. Developer options will now appear in the System section of your settings.

Access the scientific calculator

To access the scientific calculator, simply open the calculator App and rotate the phone to landscape mode. The calculator will automatically change to a scientific one.

Turn off App update notifications

If you would prefer not to be told every time an Application has been updated, open the Play Store and swipe from left to right. Then select Settings and untick the Notifications options.

Quickly access quick settings

If you want to access your quick settings more quickly, then instead of swiping down with one finger, then use two.

This should take you straight to the quick settings, however it may not work on all phones and models.

Use your device as a pedometer to track movements

There is a great app called Moves by a company called Protogeo that makes use of your devices accelerometer to record your movements, whether by walking, cycling or running. Go to the Play Store and search for Moves.

Speed up your phone

To speed up your phone, you can turn off screen animations. Go to Settings – Developer options.

Then scroll down to Window animation scale and select that. From here you can choose to turn Animations Off. This will make screen transitions faster.

Note: Developer Options is not enabled by default. To enable, go to Settings – About Device. Then tap on Build number 7 times.

How to display Owner Info on Lock Screen

Android now has a way to display your name, phone or email on your lock screen. Perfect if you have lost or misplaced your device.

To enable this go to Settings – Personal – Lock screen and security – Show information – Owner information.

Here you can enter any information you want, such as your name or email address.

Open web pages in a new tab

To open a web page in a new tab, find a link on a web page. Then press on it and then choose to open the site in a new tab.

Add email or phone number from text

To add an email or phone number to your contacts from a text message, you can long-press on the email / phone number. Then select Add to contacts

How to take a screenshot

To take a screen shot, hold down the Volume Down and Power Buttons together (i.e. exactly the same time).

This will save the current screen to your phone's memory card. They will be stored in the folder /Device Storage/Pictures/Screenshots. You can get to this folder by going to your My Files App.

Enable auto App updates

Android has a feature allowing you to update Applications automatically. This is turned off by default, but you can turn it on.

Open the Play Store App and press the Menu icon in the top left of the App. Then select Settings and in Notification section you can turn Auto-update apps on.

From here you can chose to do this over WiFi only or using your Data connection.?

How to setup blocking mode / do not disturb

If you find yourself woken up by notifications, text messages or incoming calls, then there is a handy feature called Blocking mode.

To enable this go to Settings – Device – Sounds and notifications – Do not disturb.

From here you can set a From and To time in which to block these notifications.

You can also allow notifications through from certain contacts that you don't mind bothering you.

Share / upload videos to media services like Facebook or YouTube

To share or upload a video to services like Facebook or YouTube, simply go to your Video App and long press on a video.

Then select Share via. From here you will be given options to share the video with various services.

Setting up and Access Point Name (APN) for browsing with 3G

Normally you can simply insert a SIM card and you will be able to browse the internet using 3G. Sometimes, this must be setup manually however. Before you start, you will need to ask your carrier or Telco for your APN settings.

Once you have those, go to Settings – Connections – Mobile networks – Access Point Names.

From here press the Plus sign at the top right and select New APN. Then fill in the details your carrier gave you. Then press the menu button and press Save.

Hide the content of lock screen notifications

Having notifications come through on the lock screen can be handy because you don't have to unlock your phone to see what the notification is about.

The problem with this is that someone may see the content of a notification (a text message for example) which you would like to keep private.

To change this setting to only display that the notification has arrive (rather than the actual content), then go to Settings – Sounds and notifications.

Then under the Notifications section, select Notifications on lock screen.

Select Hide content to only show the notification and not the content itself.

You can also select to turn Lock screen notification 'ON or OFF' from this menu.

Take photos while recording video

With the recent versions of Android you can now take photos while recording video by simply pressing the screen.

This will save that particular frame to the gallery while continuing to record video.

Use sound equalizer in your Music App

Android now comes with a sound Equaliser so you can adjust your bass and treble.

Simply open a music file using the Music Player App. Then go to Settings – SoundAlive and select Custom.

Then simply drag the sliders up and down to adjust the bass and treble.

Manually close an application

Android manages your applications so if the phone is running low on memory, it will close the oldest running App.

If you do need to manually close an application go to Settings – Applications – Application manager. Then swipe the screen from right to left until you are on the Running screen.

Then choose the application you want to stop and select Force Stop.

Remove homescreen widgets

To delete or remove homescreen widgets, simply press and hold. Then drag the widget to the top-right corner of the screen and into the Trash icon.

How to clear browser history, cache and cookies

If you have been browsing websites that you would prefer other people to not know about, then it's relatively simply to clear your browsing history.

Open the browser and press the Menu or More buttons at the top. Then Privacy – Delete personal data. From here you can select whether to clear the cache, cookies, passwords and more.

To avoid this extra work, you can browser in Incognito mode.

This feature does not let your browser record your browser history.

To enable this feature simply open your Browser App and press the Tabs icon at the bottom or top, depending on your browser.

Then select New secret tab or select Open Incognito Tab.

Reformat a column while browsing

If you are browsing and have zoomed in or out and the column you're reading doesn't fit the screen properly, you can pinch to zoom in. Then double tap on the column. The column will then be reformatted to fit the screen width.

Use Talkback accessibility feature

Android has an interesting new feature called Talkback which is designed for blind and low vision users.

The feature is an interesting way to navigate your phone however.

Simply go to Settings – Personal – Accessibility – Talkback to activate it.

Then your phone will give you an ongoing narration of its various functions.

How to copy photos to your PC

To copy photos to your computer, plug the device in via a USB cable. (you might have to install your device's software or drivers first).

Then locate the new drive on your PC. Go to the /DCIM/Camera/ folder Your photos will be stored there.

This may vary slightly between devices, however once you have opened the device's drive, you can do a quick search for .jpg files which will show you where your photos are located.

Some phones do not allow data transfer to PC, to enable this feature go to Settings – Developer Options – Networking and then tap on USB configuration and change it from Charging to MTP.

Note: Developer Options is not always enabled by default. To enable, go to Settings – System – About Device. Then tap on Build number 7 times to enable this secret option.

Stop YouTube videos from being blurry

If you are browsing YouTube videos on your phone and they appear blurry, then this is usually because of your connection speed.

If you are using 3G / 4G and you're in an area of low signal strength, then YouTube will sometimes automatically reduce the quality of the video. Unfortunately this can make the video very pixilated and of poor quality.

If you are using the standard Android browser, then when the video is in full screen, press the back button. Then press HQ and start playing it again.

If you are using another browser, then press the Settings icon on the bottom right of the YouTube video. Then change the quality.

This may improve the quality, but it may also lead to buffering issues.

Another solution is to use a WiFi connection, if one is available.

Resize homescreen widgets

If you want to resize your homescreen widgets, then press and hold on a widget for 2 seconds. If the widget is resizable, then an outline will appear around the widget. Simply drag the sides to resize the widget.

If the outline doesn't appear or you can't drag the lines, then the widget is a fixed sized widget.

How to play Flappy Bird on Android Lollipop

Google have hidden a clone of an Octopus inside of the Android Oreo OS.

To access this follow these instructions:
Drag down the notifications screen and go to Settings. Then scroll down to About device. Then tap on the Android version option 5 times.

You should now see a Lollipop on the screen or a double layer Oreo for Android 8.1.

Keep pressing the Lollipop/Oreo and after awhile a flying Octopus will appear.

You may need to long press on the Lollipop if multiple presses doesn't work.

You can drag and fling that Octopus all around your screen. The eight tentacles represented 8.0

Add Apps into Folders

If you like your Apps neatly sorted into folders, then there is a simple way to accomplish this.

First find the first App you would like in a folder. Then choose a second App. Press and hold on the second App and drag it over the top of the first App. They will both combine into a folder.

You can repeat this process to add more. Once you have done this grouping, you can give specific name to that folder. For that just open the folder (containing different apps), and tap on Unnamed Folder tab and add your desired name.

How to save battery life

Android now comes with some great battery management built into the OS.

Pull down your notifications screen and select Settings. Then go to Battery and you will see some useful stats such as the time remaining. There are also two other options: Power saving mode and Ultra power saving mode. Select one of these to really make your phone last the distance.

Be warned that these can limit your device quite considerably.

You can also increase Battery Life by minimizing the numbers of Apps running in the background.

Useful widget to close all running Apps

Your phone comes with a handy widget which lets you kill all running tasks. This is great if you want to quickly free up some memory.

To use the widget, press and hold for 2 seconds on a blank part of any homescreen. Then find the Active Apps Manager widget and install it.

Once that is done, press the widget and it will show you all currently running Apps. Press End all to close all running Apps.

How to fix - this player does not support this type of audio file error

There are a number of solutions to this error. Go through the following steps:

Go to Settings – Applications – Application manager. Then swipe right to left to go to All (along the top). Then find the App called Media

Storage. Click on that and select Force Close. Then select Clear Data. (warning: this will delete the cache for your media player so you may lose things such as recently played, most played etc. But you will not lose your music).

Next, go back to list of Apps and find Music Player. Again, press Force Close and then Clear Data.

Once that's done, go to the Play Store and download an App called Re Scan Media and run it. Wait 5 minutes for the device to re-scan your media.

If you still cannot play your music, then try turning your phone off and removing your SDCard / memory card (if you have one). Then turn the phone on without the card. Then turn it off again and reinsert the card. Finally turn it on again with the card back in.

If you still can't play music, then some users have said that there may be a conflict with the Twitter App. Try uninstalling this and see if the error persists.

You can also try downloading some new media player from Play Store and try running media on this new player.

Turn off camera shutter sound

If you don't want to hear the shutter sound when you take photos, then there are a few things you can try.

Firstly, some countries have laws to force the phone to play these sounds. Assuming you're not in one of these countries, then the first thing you can try is to go to the Camera App – Settings – Shutter Sound – Off.

If that doesn't work, then you can try turning the volume of the phone down or put it in silent mode when taking photos.

The last option is to Root your phone. If you don't know what that means, then it's best not to attempt it unless you have thoroughly read about the process. Once Rooted, go to this folder on your phone: /system/media/audio/ui and rename the camerashutter and/or cameraclick OGG files to something else.

Alternatively, on a rooted phone you can use a Root Browser, to edit /system/csc/feature.xml and set the option to TRUE. Then you should be able to go to Camera App – Settings – Shutter Sound – Off.

Bypass the Lock screen at home

Locking your phone is a great security feature, but when you're at home it's normally not necessary.

A featured called Trusted Places enables you to bypass the lock screen when you're at specific geographic places.

To set it up go to Settings – Lock screen and security – Smart lock – Trusted places. You can also set up the bypass to work when your phone is connected to specific Bluetooth devices such as Smart watches or Audio devices.

You can also override this (i.e. lock your screen when it is at the location). To override, just press and hold the padlock icon on the lock screen.

This may not work on all phones, models or networks.

Save images in browser, email or text

To save an image in an email or in the browser, long press on the image and a menu will appear allowing you to save it.

For images inside text messages, you might have to press and hold on the message itself, rather than the image.

How to close Apps

Android manages Apps very well and some Apps do not have the option to close them specifically. Normally the App will stay running in the background and only close when many other Apps have been opened.

If you do want to close or terminate an App, then press and hold the Multitasking key on your phone. On some devices you may need to long press the Home key. Then you can swipe the Apps off the screen to close them.

Even after doing that, there may be some apps still running in the background.

To close these apps, go to Settings and open Application icon, from here you can open applications list and tap on any app you want to close.

From here simply tap on force stop and application will stop working in background.

Remove a whole text message conversation

If you want to remove an entire text message thread, go into Messages and look for the thread. Then long press on it and select Delete thread

Quickly search for a contact

There are a couple of ways to bring up one of your contacts.

First, while in your Contacts App, simply start typing in the search bar at the top of the screen.

Or else a quicker method is to use the Google Search widget (installed by long pressing on a vacant part of your homescreen and installing the widget) and start typing the name of the contact you want to dial. This will quickly filter the correct contact.

Set voicemail number / password

To set your voicemail number which allows your phone to automatically input your voicemail password, then open your Dialler App.

Then press the More or Menu button and choose Call settings. Then scroll down to Voicemail settings and set a Voicemail number (you might need to check with your carrier for the correct number).

Depending on your carrier you may have to enter the series of steps required to go through the voicemail menu, for example: *86,,yourpassword# (a comma inserts a pause).

How to find your MAC address

If you want to find your phone's WiFi MAC address (for improved WiFi security), then go to Settings – System – About device – Status.

Then scroll down until you see WiFi MAC Address. The address should be a series of Hex numbers and letters.

Add photos to contacts

First open your Contacts App and select a contact. Then press Edit at the top of the screen.

Then should then see some options to either take a photo or select a photo from your Gallery.

To enable this feature, make sure the contact is saved in the Phone memory.

Copy files between your phone and PC over WiFi

To copy files between your phone and PC, go to the Android Play Market and download an app called Air Droid.

This is an extremely useful App that connects your phone to your PC wirelessly, allowing you to move files and many, many other things.

Alternatively if you just want to copy using USB then simply plug a micro USB cable into your phone and it should appear as another drive on your PC.

Some phones do not allow data transfer to PC, to enable this feature go to Settings – Developer Options – Networking, and then tap on USB configuration and change it from 'Charging' to 'MTP'.

Note: Developer Options is not always enabled by default. To enable, go to Settings – System – About Device. Then tap on Build number 7 times to enable this secret option.

How to unmount SD card

If you would like to unmount your SD card for whatever reason, then drag down your notifications menu from the top of the screen and press the Settings icon.

Then find Storage – SD card – Unmount SD card.

How to change to a better keyboard

While the stock standard keyboard is fine, there are much better keyboards available. First, you need to go to the Play Store and download one.

Try searching for the word 'keyboard' and you will see a number of options.

One of the best keyboards is a keyboard called Swiftkey, which is a top-rate App. This will literally change the way you feel about your phone as the standard keyboard can be quite a frustrating experience.

Download your chosen keyboard and go through any install steps that you are presented with.

If you see a warning saying the keyboard will collect all information (including credit cards) just ignore this. This is just a security feature that Android shows for every third-party keyboard that you install.

Then, go to the App you want to type in. You should now see a little Keyboard icon on the row at the bottom of your screen, towards the bottom-right corner. Press that icon and you can switch between all of the keyboards you have installed.

Quickly access notifications from lock screen

To see notifications on your Lock screen, the best option is to download an App called NoLed from the Play Store. This will show notifications such as text messages, emails and missed calls as bright icons on your homescreen.

You can choose between very small squares or small icons and these can assigned by coloured.

Printed in Great Britain
by Amazon